Who Fails As An Artist …?
…One who loves his paintings

Copyright reserved 2018
Magunta Venkata Subba Reddy (alias Magunta Dayakar)

Other Books on Art

How To Start A Painting And How To Plan It ?
How To Finish A Painting ?
Painting Landscapes From Imagination
Learn Composition and Create Beautiful Paintings
Simplified Color Schemes for Art Students
Capturing Movement in portrait Painting

Contents

This book is my master piece like Behrman's painted leaf. ... 3
Chapter One ... 4
   You should know the reasons for your failures ... 5
   Examples of how language of art works in painting ... 7
      Example 1 - Something is not right ... 8
      Example 2 - Whether painting is good or not ... 9
      Example 3 - Call it a crippled painting ... 10
      Example 4 - It will become static ... 11
      Example 5 - Not that much effective ... 12
   It's a mind game ... 13
   Visual Mind ... 15
      Example 1 - Brush Strokes ... 17
      Example 2 - Replacement of an object in your interiors ... 18
Chapter Two ... 19
   I will tell you a story ... 20
   Let us find the answers for these questions ... 23
   Your painting won't be realistic. Why? ... 26
      Example – Creative Eye ... 29
Chapter Three ... 31
   Rather than loving it ... 32
   One incident in a small-time artist's life ... 35
   Understanding - Not Love ... 42
   Why artists paint? ... 44
My last words ... 47
About Magunta Dayakar ... 49

Page is intentionally blank

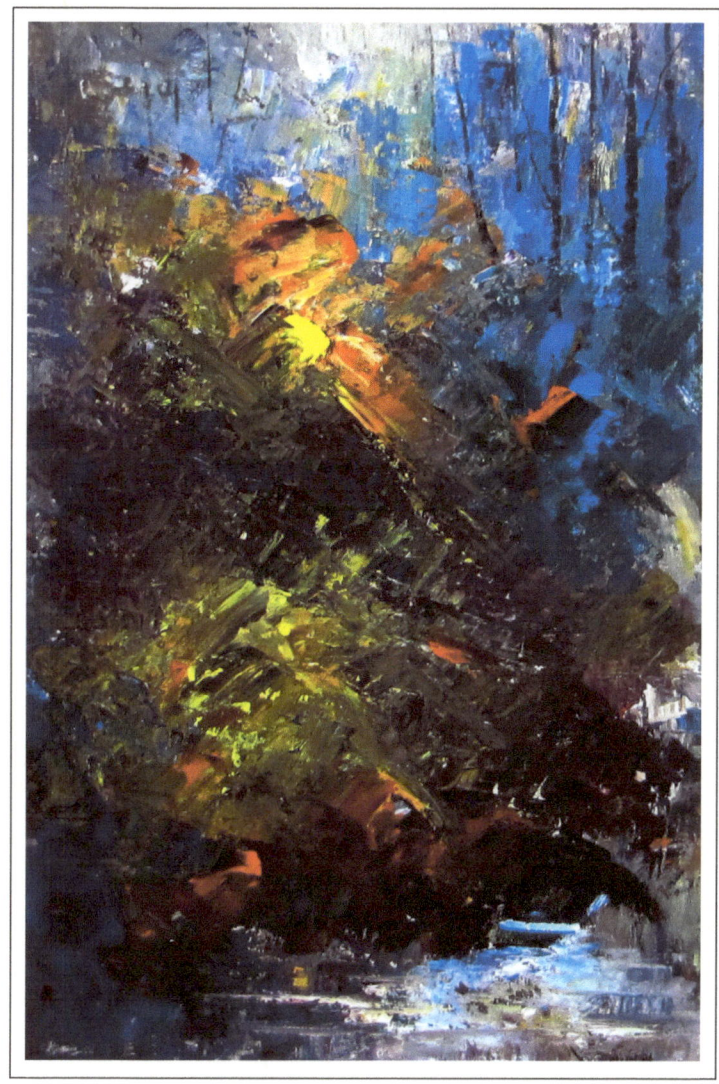

Artist : Magunta Dayakar Acrylics on Canvas

The basic purpose of all art is to relax people who are stressed out with day to day survival. If any art is not achieving this purpose then how can we call it art?

This book is my master piece like Behrman's painted leaf…

This is my seventh book. This is my master piece like Behrman's painted last leaf on the wall in the story of 'The Last Leaf.'

In my childhood, I read American writer O. Henry's short story ' The Last Leaf '. In that story a young woman Johnsy is seriously ill with pneumonia. She believes that when the ivy vine on the wall outside her window loses all its leaves, she will also die. Everyday a leaf drops from the vine. Behrman, an old artist, who lives in the basement of the same apartment, always used to say that one day he will paint his master piece, came to know Johnsy's belief about the last leaf of the ivy vine. He paints a leaf in that rainy night on the wall with perfect realism as if it is a real leaf where ivy vine lies. The next morning when Johnsy saw that last leaf did not fall from the ivy wine, she starts to recover from her illness but Behrman, who caught pneumonia while painting the leaf, dies. But he painted his master piece which saved a life.

This story inspired me a lot. As an artist and writer, I always dreamt of painting a master piece like Behrman's painted leaf. This book is my Painted leaf.

After creating a master piece like this at the fag end of my life, there is nothing left to excite me to write any more. All my previous books dealt with technical aspects of color, composition, imagination and portrait painting. But this book is different, rather than concentrating on technical aspects of painting like my other books, this book focuses on understanding painting. This is about what one should do to become a true artist.

I hope this short book will inspire you to get in depth insight in both art and life.

Chapter One

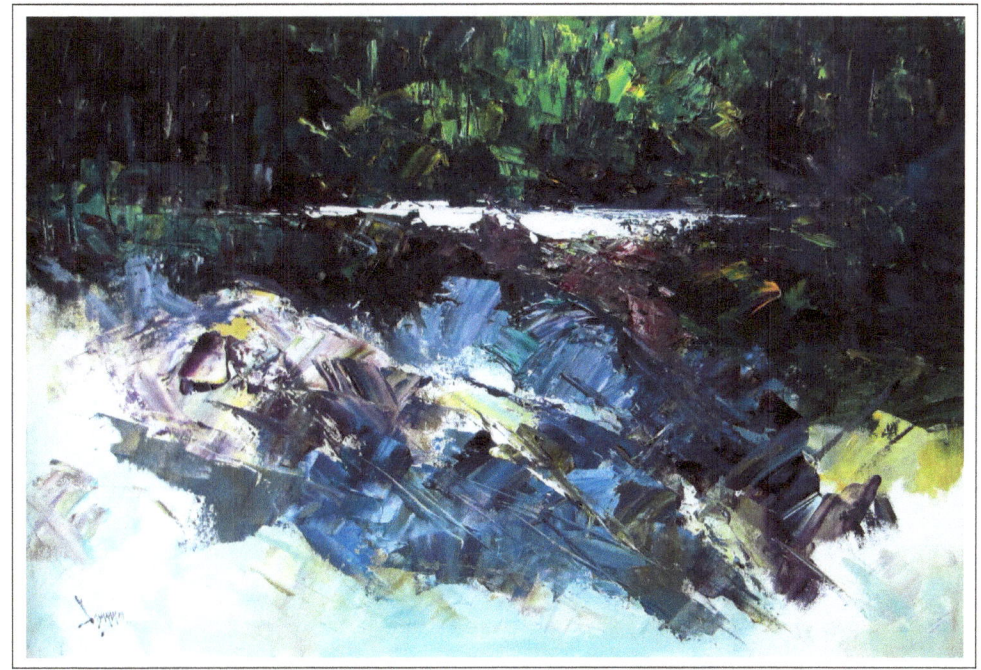

Artist : Magunta Dayakar   Acrylics on Canvas

It's easy to conquer the enemy who exists outside rather than the one who is inside. Your enemy is your urge to paint well.

You should know the reasons for your failures

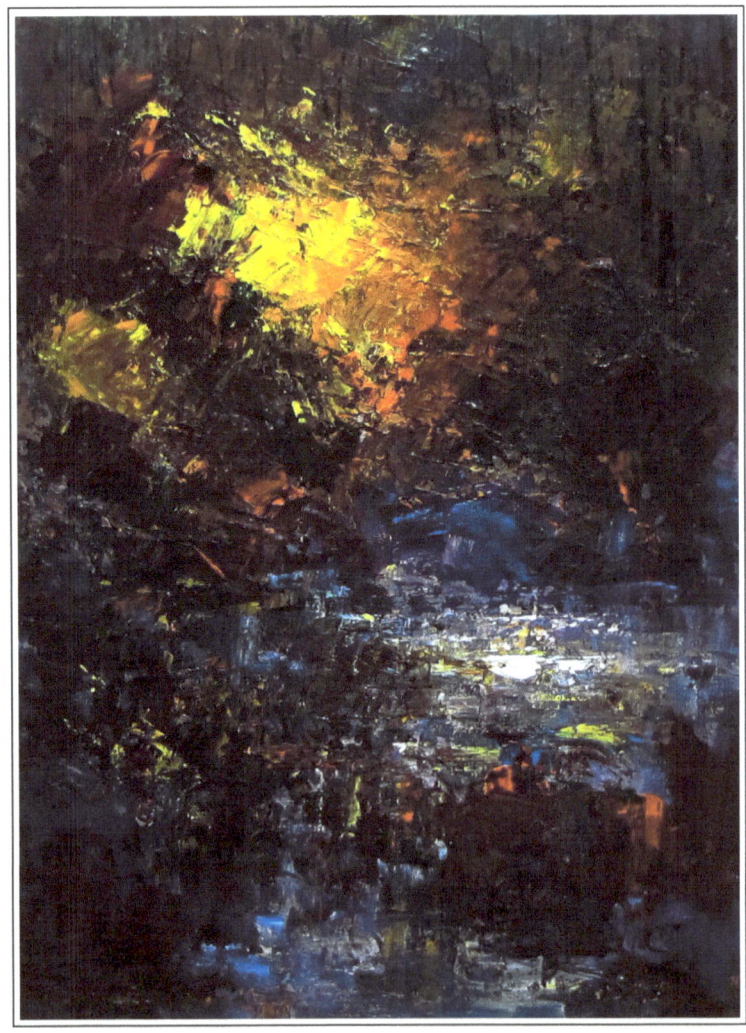

Artist : Magunta Dayakar   Acrylics on Canvas

He is an artist. I know him well. Very hard working. Having a lot of passion for art. A simple human being. Never bothered about luxuries.

The only problem with him is he didn't learn language of art and he is not interested to learn it either.
Because he believes in Intuition. 'With intuition you could do anything.' That's what he believes. Sometimes his paintings turn out well. Sometimes not. He would give a reason for that. He used to say, "Art is like that. Sometimes our intuition may not be in our favour."

I tried a few times to change his notion about intuition and the language of art.
I tried telling him, " Intuition will come to us from our experiences of life. For doing paintings we should know the language of art. You have got an intuition from your experiences of life. You didn't learn language of art. Because of that sometimes your paintings don't turn out well. And you don't know reason for your failure also. "

He became angry at my words. But he controlled himself with some effort and said, " I don't believe all this nonsense. Artist doesn't need to bother about language of art. Intuition is enough to do paintings well. "

I didn't argue with him. Simply I became silent. Usually I won't try to convince anybody with my opinions. Because he is my friend, that's why I tried to make him understand certain things. But it was futile.
If you are an artist, you should know the reasons for your failures. If you are unable to know the reasons for your failure, you are not able to correct them. Then you won't have consistency in your work. When you are inconsistent, you are not a professional. If you are not a professional, you won't survive financially. If you are not bothered about earning money for livelihood from your art, then it's different.
The problem with these kind of artists is that they don't bother exploring the subject in depth. They just believe that they have a creative mind, with that they can paint anything successfully.

They love their paintings very much, no doubt about it. But they are ignorant about the language of art. They don't know that painting is a mind game. To play that mind game just having love for it is not enough. Having love is only a starting point. Learning language of art will help you to play that mind game.

Examples of how language of art works in painting

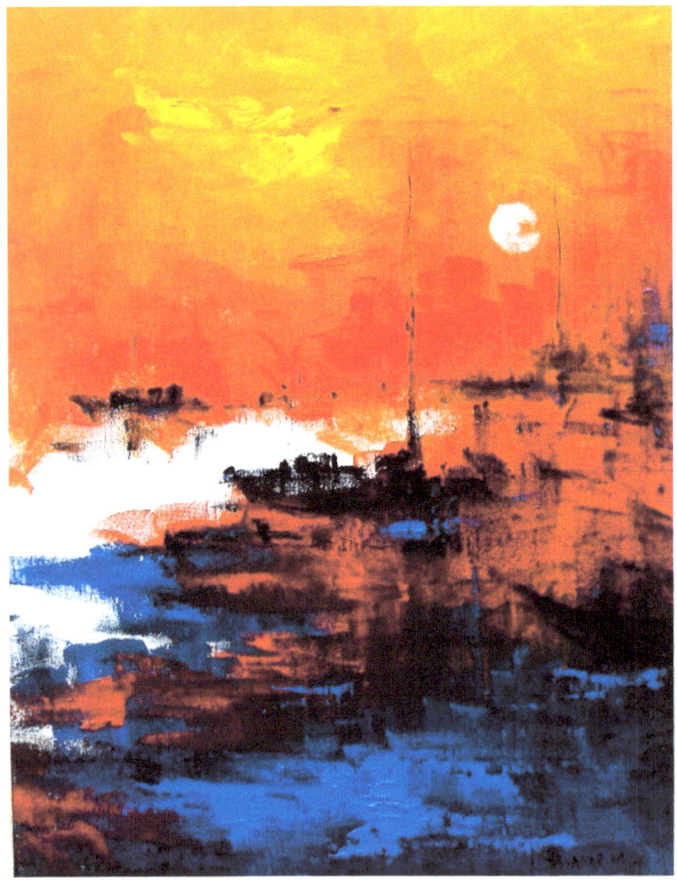

In the next few pages I will explain how I played with the language of art in painting the above picture. Study them. That will help you to understand how much of a mind game is involved in the act of painting.

Example 1 - Something is not right

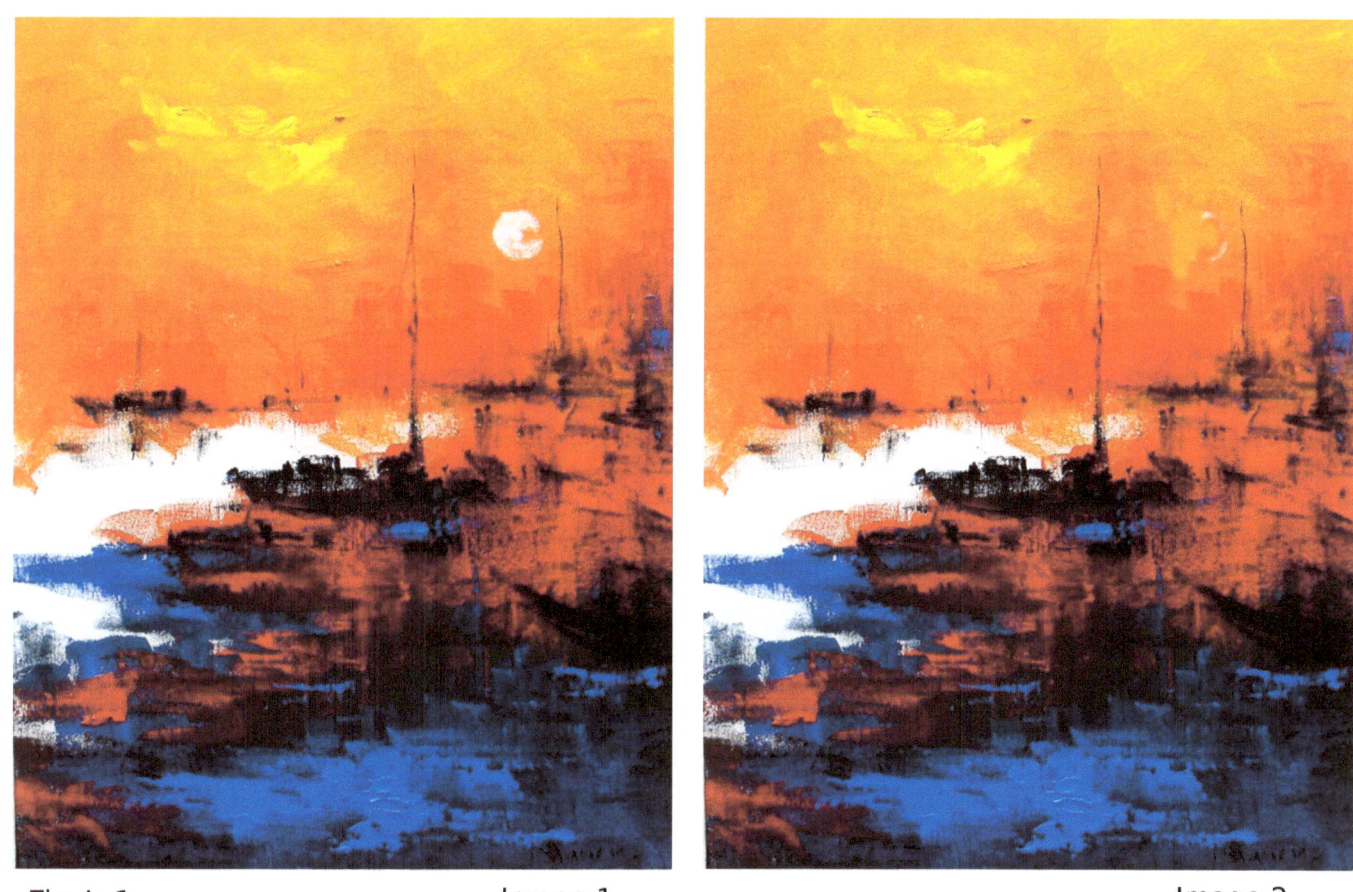

Fig L-1   Image 1   Image 2

Look at images 1 and 2 in Fig L-1. I removed white color sun in the sky. It resulted in loss of balance. It will give a feeling that something is not right. The viewer may not have knowledge in painting to analyse the reason for that problem. But he will sense it. Then he will lose interest in the painting.

Example 2 - Whether painting is good or not

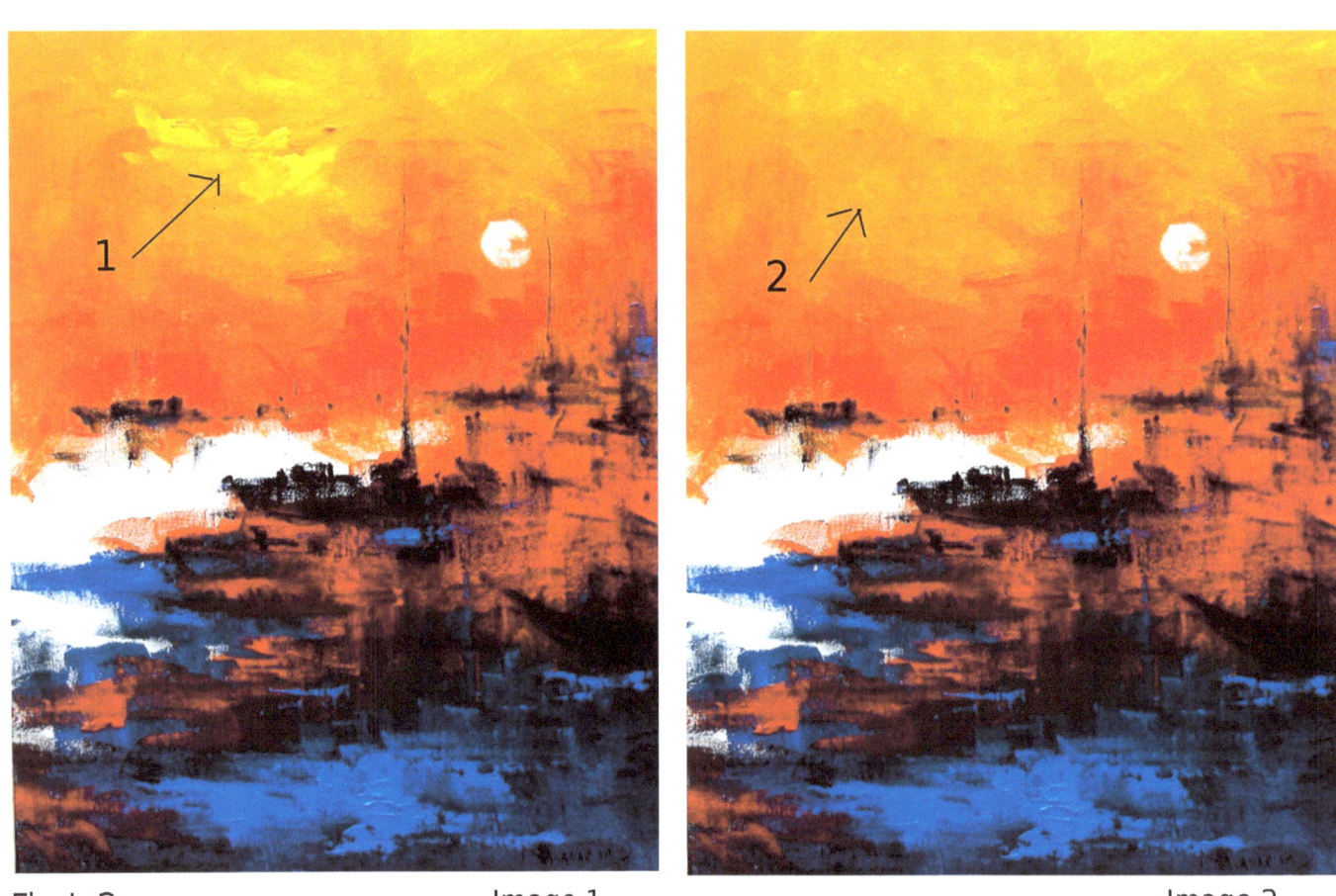

Fig L-2   Image 1   Image 2

Look at image 1 in Fig L-2. I marked bright yellow orange area with an arrow. In image 2, I removed the brightness of yellow. Analyse what happened? Observe carefully … Movement is lost in the painting to a certain extent. Result … viewer will get confused about whether painting is good or not.

Example 3 - Call it a crippled painting

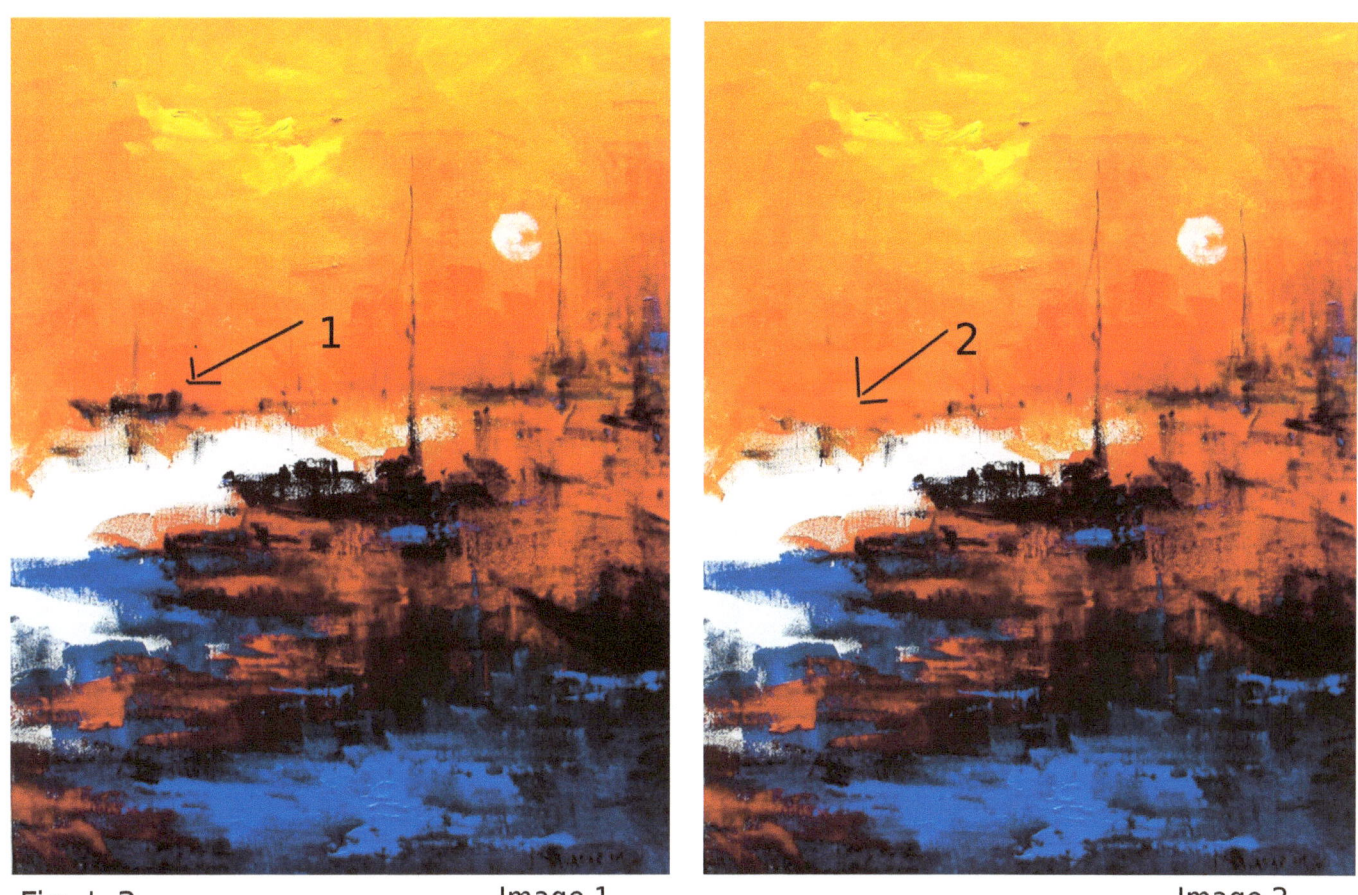

Fig L-3   Image 1   Image 2

Look at image 1 in Fig L-3. A small boat is there. I painted it for the balance on the left side. In image 2 I removed it (Marked as no.2). It results in loss of balance and disrupts movement also. When balance and movement is lost, rhythm, harmony and unity also will be lost. You call it a crippled painting.

Example 4 - It will become static

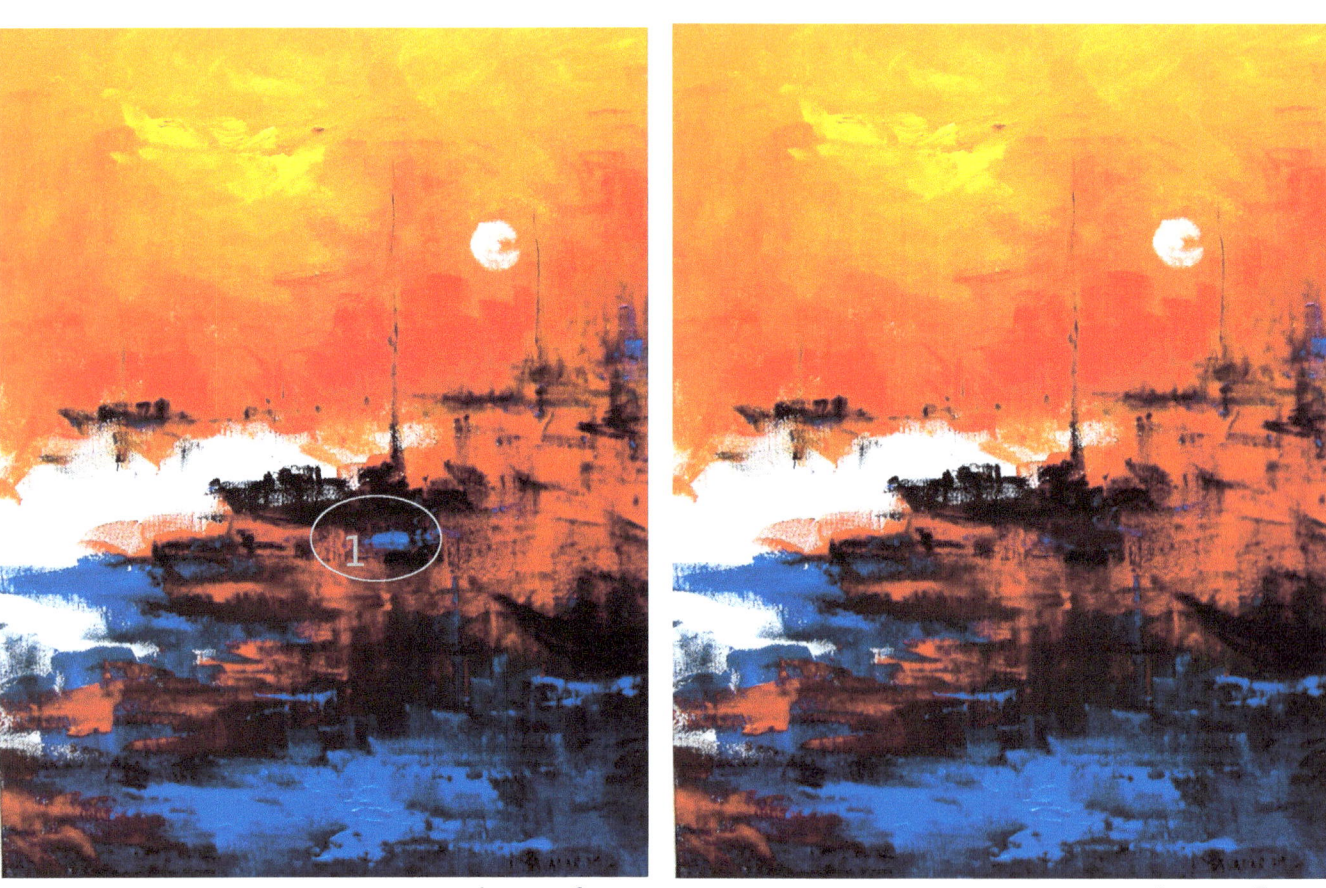

Fig L-4   Image 1   Image 2

Look at the image 1 in Fig L-4, where an area is circled below the boat. There you can see a small blue streak. I removed it in image 2. See what happened. That small blue was connecting the lower half with the upper half. When it is removed, picture has been crippled. It lost energy. Remember … Energy is movement. When energy is lost, movement is lost as well. When it loses movement, picture becomes static.

Example 5 - Not that much effective

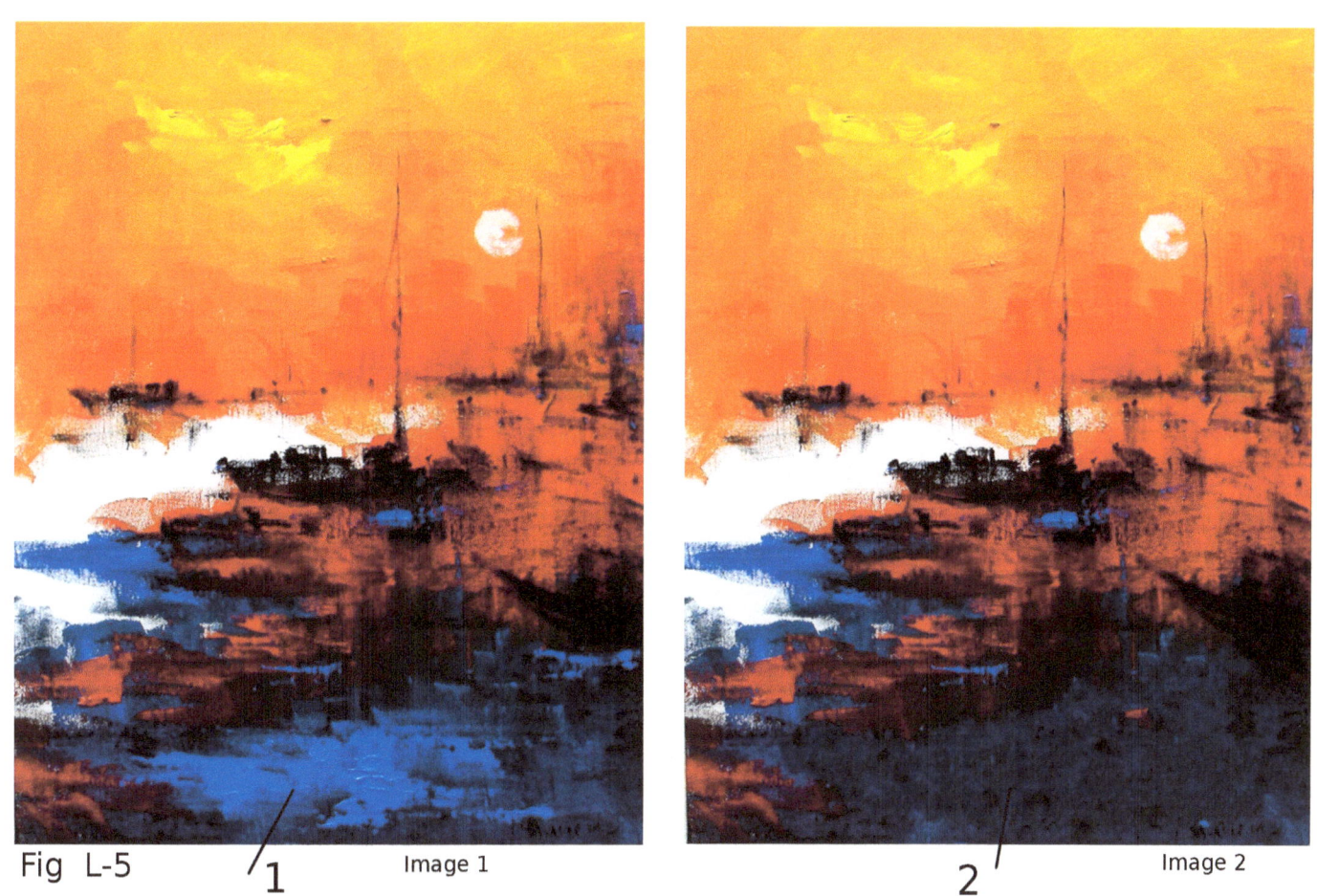

Fig L-5 /1 Image 1   2/ Image 2

Look at the image 1 in Fig L-5. Observe where I marked no.1, that area has blue violet color. I removed that color in image 2. See what happened? Painting lost its color vibrancy. Not that much effective as image 1. This is the power of language of art. Whenever you are applying language of art in your painting, purely it's a mind game. To play this mind game effectively you should be good at the language of art.

It's a mind game

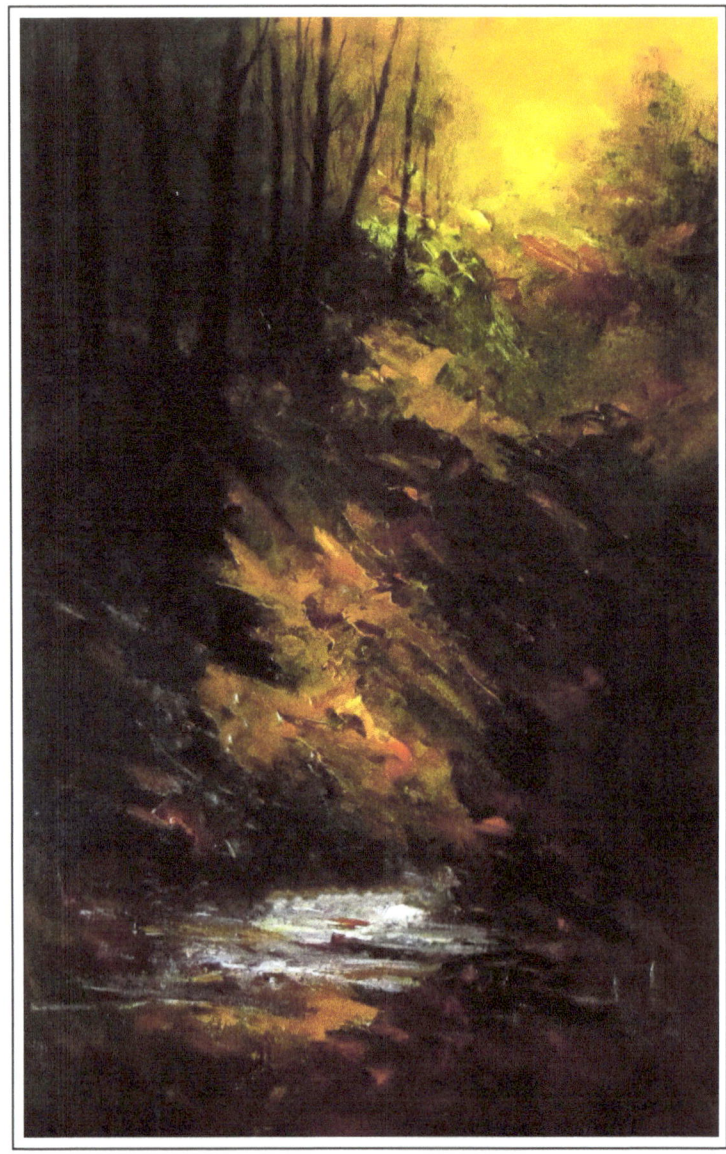

Artist : Magunta Dayakar   Acrylics on Canvas

See this painting. How is it? I have done this to enjoy the fun of doing painting. Yes. Doing painting is fun, if you have understood the language of art. Painting is fun if we know what we are doing and what we have to do. What I have realized while doing painting is, it's a mind game.

When I wrote fiction, I used to visualize my fictitious world, the people in it, their interactions, their movements, consequences, how the characters, incidents evolve and move towards climax, in between so many ambiguities, anxieties, uncertainties, frustrations and depressions, everything leading to climax. Once the climax is over there is a terrific relaxation, elation, finally fun.

The entire process I call it a mind game. I believe this mind game happens in every creative act whether it is writing, painting, music, dance, acting. The same way when I start painting, I have a rough idea in my mind of what I want to see on the canvas, my brush moves on canvas to give clarity for that rough image, then … shapes will form, light illuminates them, colors interact with each other as bright and dull tones, relations will be established as values, temperature will be analysed with each and every plane, balance can be observed, variety, repetition, contrast will be adjusted, edges will be blurred, softened, sharpened … every brush stroke should interact with the whole canvas, finally ending with a check of movement, harmony and unity. That's the painting.

Simply it's a mind game. It's easy to conquer the enemy who is existing outside rather than the one who is in your inside. Here the enemy is your urge to paint well. To satisfy that urge you should acquire the tools of language of art. With the help of those tools along with your intuition you will be able to win the mind game.

These tools are …. Sketch, Value, Color and Composition. Here the crucial thing is knowing composition is different from applying it. Once you start applications mind game also starts. Truly it's a mind game. To play a mind game you need a visual mind.

Visual Mind

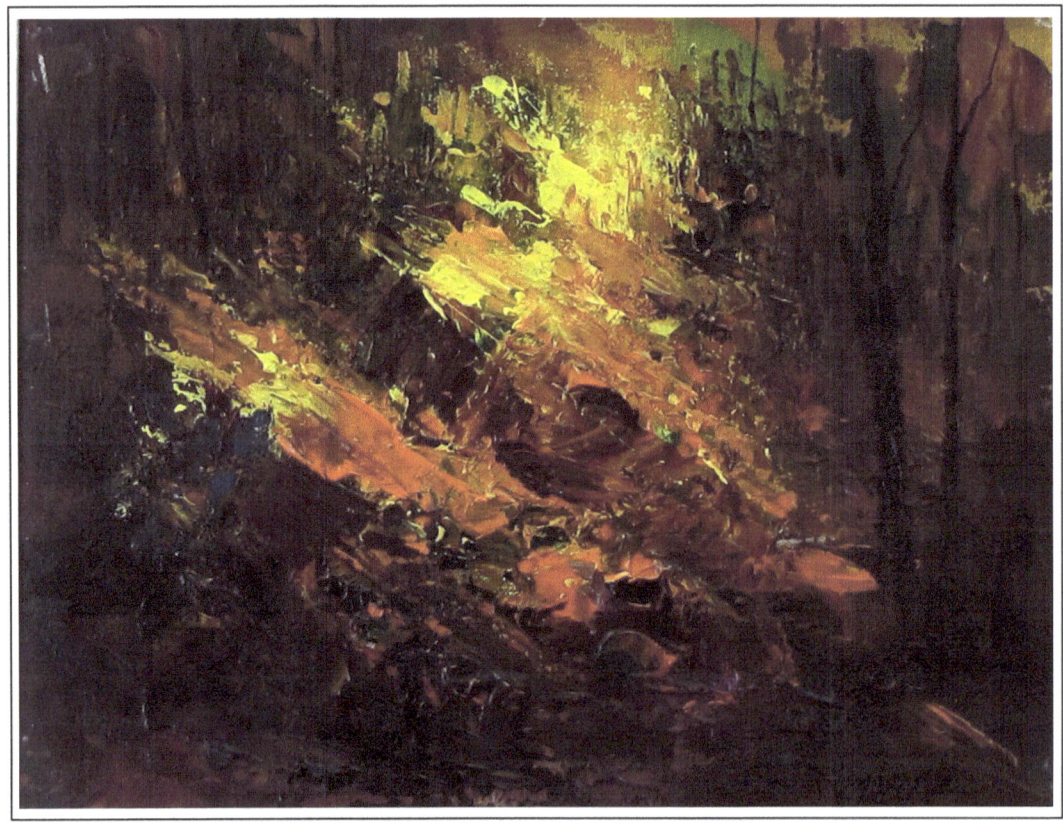

Artist : Magunta Dayakar   Acrylics on Canvas

" … Visual mind! What is it sir? " One of my students asked me.

" I don't like giving theoretical explanations, which will confuse you. I will explain it to you in simple words. For example, when you go to a decorative items shop to buy some object for your house, if you find something you like, automatically you are able to judge whether it will suit your interiors or not. In that moment you are able to see interior space of your house in your mind. That is visual mind. We all have it but we use it in limited areas only. To be a successful painter we should apply it in our painting.

For example, when you are making a brush stroke on the canvas you should know how it will connect with other strokes which you have already made. But the problem is when you are applying a brush stroke you won't able to see the remaining brush strokes on the canvas at that moment. But the visual mind can do that job for you. It's just like the way visual mind works when you are buying an object and judging whether it suits your interiors or not (See Fig V-1 && V-2 in next pages).

Think about it. When your visual mind is working in decorative items shop why don't you make it work in your painting? You have to make it work. To be a successful artist you need this. You call this skill "Visual Imagination".

" … Visual Imagination? " she asked in a questioning manner.

" Yes. Visual Imagination. If you develop visual mind it will lead to visual imagination. To be a successful artist you should practice it."

"Is it not a special skill? Is it possible to achieve it through practice? "

"It's not at all a special skill. It can be learned through practice… To create Reality in your paintings it will be the key thing along with language of painting."

" Reality? When we are painting something from life or photographs, is it not reality? Especially when they are looking life like ..."

" Not at all …"

After a few moments silence she said … " It's confusing."

" I will tell you a story, it will clear your confusion about what is reality, what is not. "

She was looking at me with total attention to know what I am going to say.

Example 1 - Brush Strokes

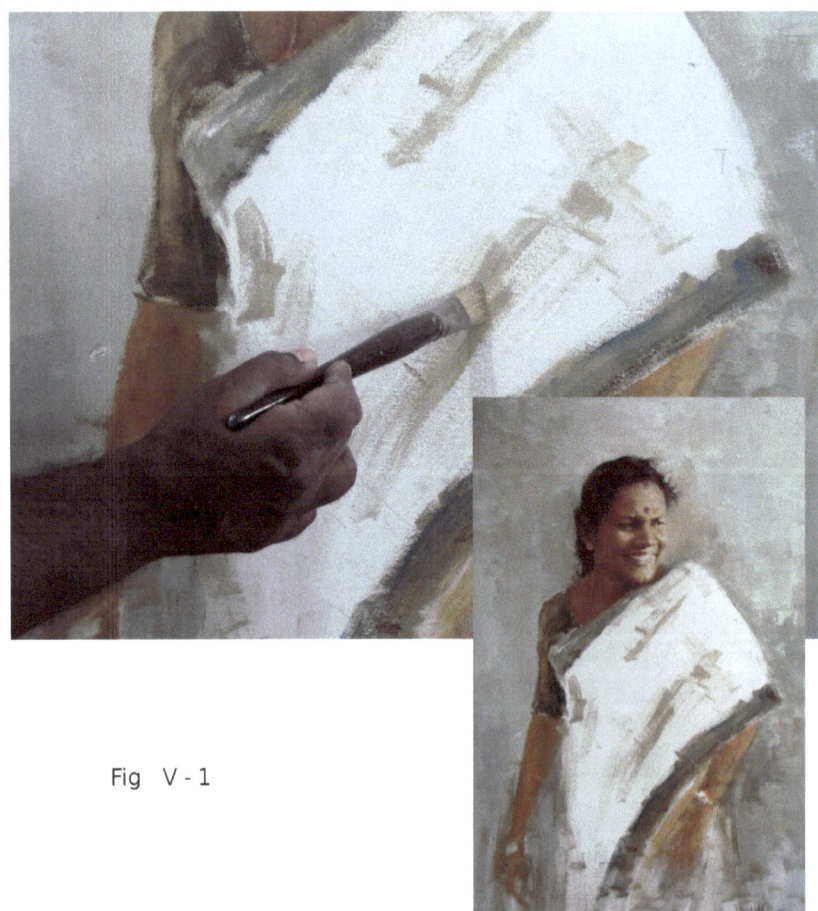

Fig V - 1

Look at this image Fig V-1. When you apply a brush stroke in one area, you have to visualise it in your mind, how it interacts with other brush strokes in the painting. You have to use your visual mind work that way.

Example 2 - Replacement of an object in your interiors

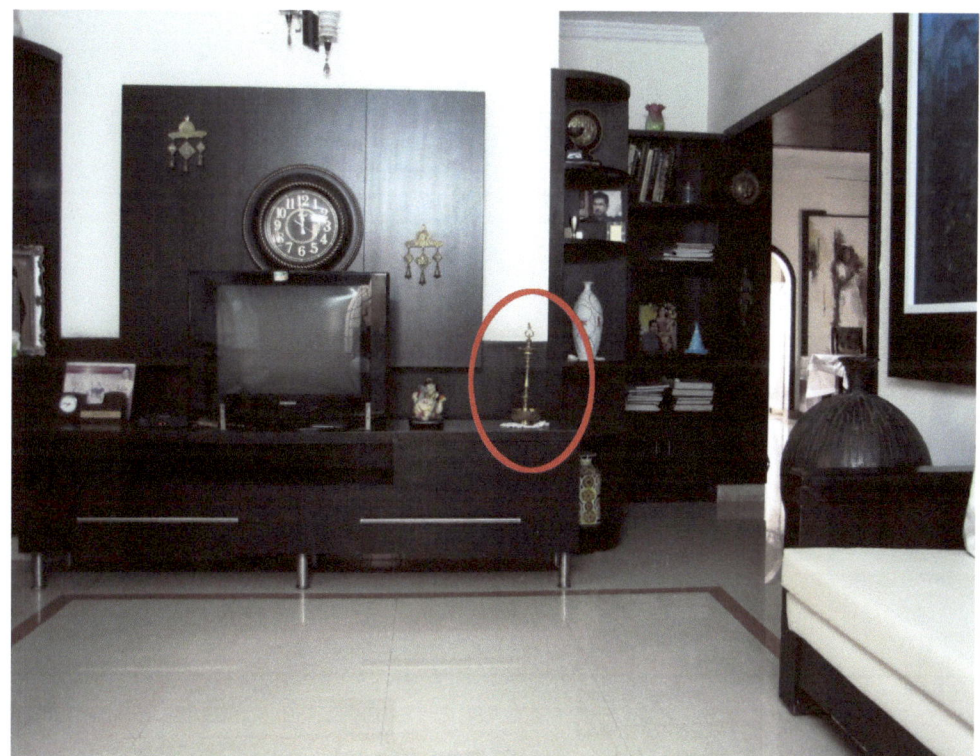

Fig V - 2

Look at the red marked area in the photograph (Fig V-2). You want to change the object in that. For that you went to a decorative articles shop. There you are able to choose the object which is suitable to replace the object in the red marked area. Everyone has this visual imagination skill. You have to use that skill when you are applying brush strokes. It's possible only if you try for it.

Chapter Two

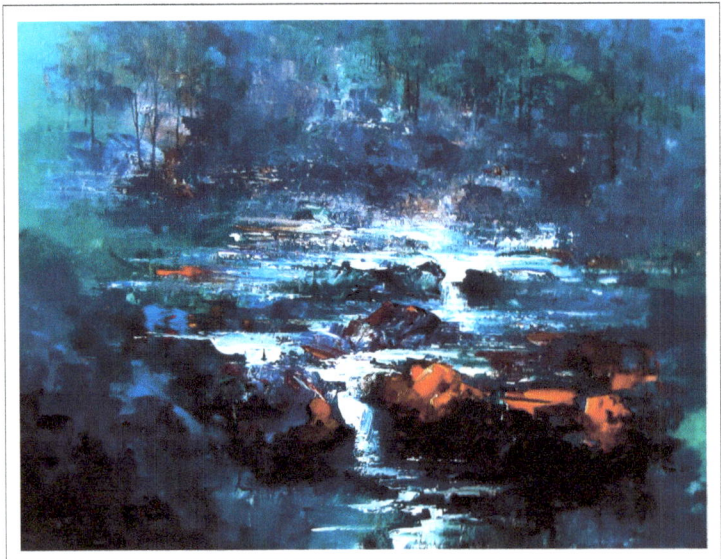

Artist : Magunta Dayakar   Acrylics on Canvas

Many people think what we are seeing is reality! Is it true? Scientifically it is not. Eyes will see everything upside down. The brain will map them to normal appearance. It's believed that for the first few days newborns see the world upside down, as their brain just hasn't learnt to flip the images yet. Is it not amazing that what we are seeing with our eyes is not real! Then what is reality?

I will tell you a story

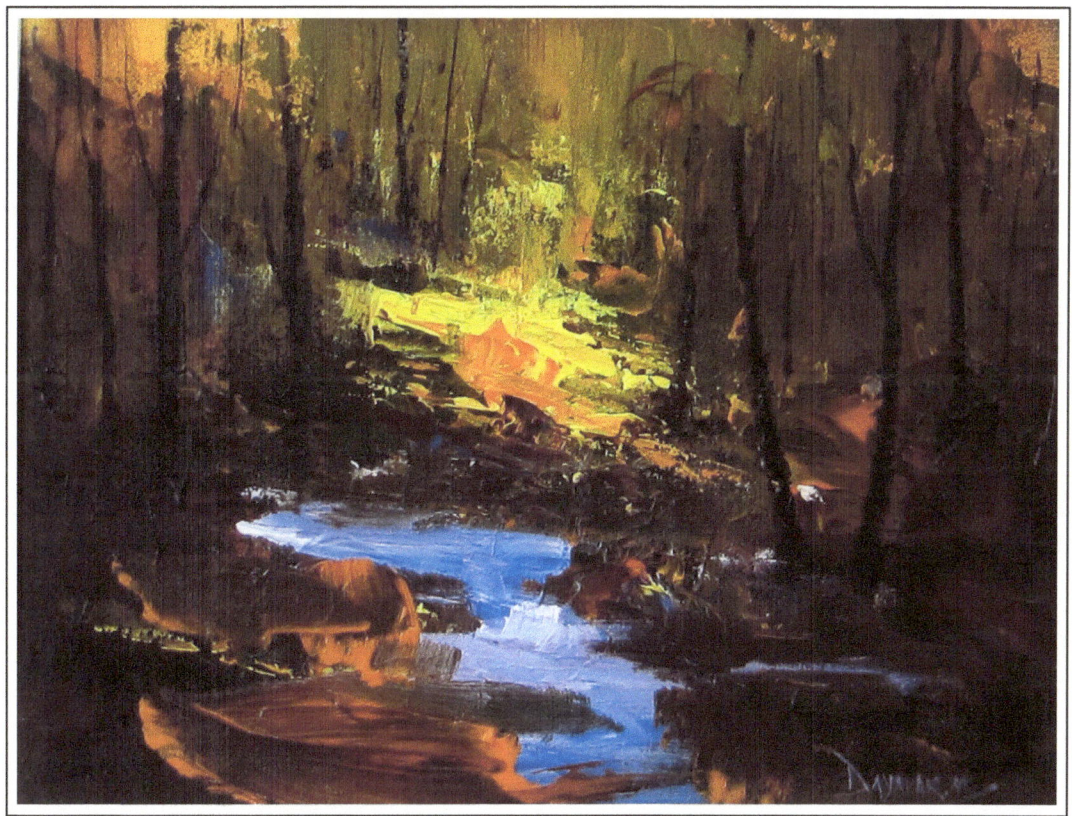

Artist : Magunta Dayakar   Acrylics on Canvas

You know that in drawing they say …' Learn to see ' What does this mean? We draw or sketch something, which is in front of us, it may be a pear, an orange, a vase, a landscape or a model. Usually we try to draw a person or a thing the way it appears to our eye.
' We will draw a person or a thing the way it appears to our eye. ' I think the key lies here.

You are seeing the model. You are trying to draw it the way it appears to your eye. You are thinking it is the right way of sketching. The muscles, the joints whatever you are seeing, you are sketching it. You are feeling a lot of joy, because you are capturing the model as it is. Perfect replication. Then you have started to think you are a good artist, that you have wonderful skills of sketching. When you show your work to others they also feel the same what you have felt. They will praise you, that you are a very talented artist. From that moment on, you will be on cloud nine. But … they are only clouds. You could not survive there for long. Fall from there is imminent. Because there is no base for you to stay. To survive you need a base. How to get that base? To get that base you have to understand what the reality truly is. How do we achieve it in our paintings?

I will narrate a story to you.
In thirteenth century there was an artist Cimabue, he was honoured as the first painter of modern times. When he was travelling through countryside he saw a boy with a lot of sheep. At the same moment he was surprised at what he saw. It was a drawing of a sheep full of life made on a flat stone. Rarely had he seen that kind of life in drawings even in the ones done by a professional artist.

" What makes this boy's drawing capture so much life? "
To know the answer for that question he started to talk with the boy. After talking for some time he got the answer, why that drawing had that much life.

The boy used to come every day to the countryside along with his sheep to feed them. Once he comes there he would forget everything, even the sheep. He used to observe everything, whatever was around him. Flowers, shrubs, bushes, stones, sky, hills, clouds and his sheep... He knew their every movement by heart. How the flowers would glitter with sunshine, how the clouds were moving in the sky, how the sheep would rest under the shadows of trees, how they move to find and eat grass, take rest, run from one place to another place ….

Slowly with time his heart was filled with those images, even in sleep he started to see them. Then one fine moment he took a piece of stone, sharpened and started to draw on the flat surface of a nearby large flat shaped stone. He had drawn everything what he knew by heart. Everything, whatever came from his heart captured life.

After knowing the boy's story, Cimabu took him to Florence to train him. Later the shepherd boy became the first Renaissance painter who introduced accurate drawing from life which is called representative art. The boy's name is Giotto. While Byzantine period ended with Cimabu, Renaissance age started with Giatto.

Now, again we will come to our question, '...What is Reality? Why Cimabu was surprised by the shepherd boy's drawing? If the camera clicks the same visuals, will it not get the same effect? The answer is '… No.'

Why? Is it not realistic whatever camera snaps? Does it not appear so? If not ...why? Then what is the true meaning of reality?

In life truth and beauty exist together. Truth is internal. Beauty is external. When you combine both external beauty and inner truth, that you call reality.

Camera picks up only the external beauty, it fails to capture inner truth. So what camera captures is half truth. How can half truth become reality?

When even camera snaps are not realistic, when they are only half truths then how were Giotto sketches realistic? What makes them different from camera snaps?

Not only artists, whoever wants to be creative they should know the answers for these. Let us find the answers for these questions...

You have started to think you are a good artist, you have wonderful skills of sketching. When you show your work to others they also feel the same what you have felt. They will praise you that you are a very talented artist. From that moment on, you will be on cloud nine. But … they are only clouds. You could not survive there for long. Fall from there is imminent. Because there is no base to stay.

Let us find the answers for these questions...

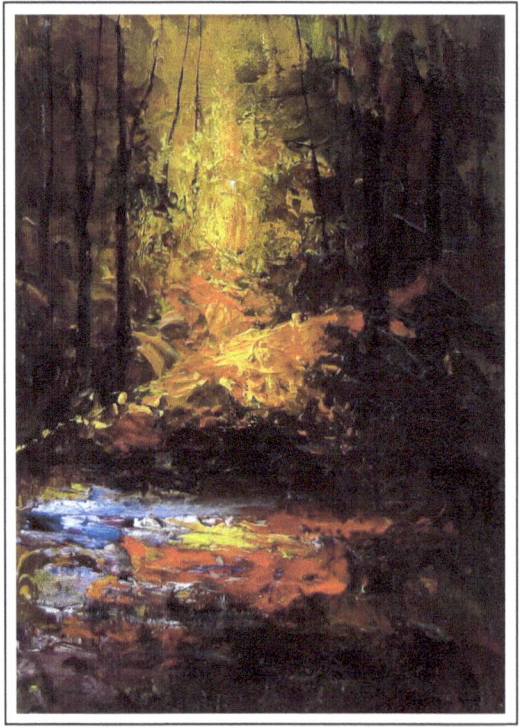

Artist : Magunta Dayakar   Acrylics on Canvas

When camera clicks a scene, a figure or anything, it is just capturing its appearance.
No more. No less.
Put this aside for a moment.

Sometimes when we are deceived or exploited by a person close to us, he may be relative, friend or business partner, we will be advised by others that we should have been more careful, that we should have studied his real character which he had hidden from us. " Before associating with him in business you should have understood his true nature." We are told like this.

That means the way that person appears to our eye is not real. He may appear to us very nice, warm and most lovable person. But when you try to know what he is thinking inside, how he behaves in different situations, then only you will understand his true character. This character may be different from his external appearance. If you combine this external appearance and internal character, then you will know about him totally. That is his real face. You also call it as … whole. This is how we should analyse our friends, our relatives and our associates if we want to know their true personalities. With camera this is not possible. It clicks only external appearances. That's why whatever you click with camera, that's not real. It will fail to capture the inner character. So it's a half truth. It's not real.

Then again, a question arises, 'If camera's image is not real, how about Giotta's drawings? Why do you say they are realistic?'

The answer is simple. He captured inner character of the sheep along with their external appearances which camera won't be able to get. It happened through his understanding about them. What is this understanding? How he achieved it?

To know the answer, let's look into Giotto's life.

He used to take the sheep to countryside every day and followed them wherever they go. Observed them, whatever they may be doing. Doing this act every day, he had understood their body language, their movements, when they will search for food, when they like to take rest, when they will run … everything about them. That way he understood not only their external structures but also their behavioural patterns. This behavioural pattern is their inner character. Knowing their inner character is understanding about them.

I will explain to you about this behavioural pattern and how it will reflect character. For example, let's say someone was murdered in the park where people walk every morning. When the walkers come into the park in the morning and come to know about it. Different people, different reactions would happen there. Someone wants to see who was murdered. Someone will avoid that spot where murdered person is lying. Another one may not come to park for a few days after that. You call these responses as behavioural patterns. These patterns are their inner character. This inner character would be built by environment influences, where they had grown up, their financial backgrounds, their family, friends and everything connected since childhood.

The same way Giotto understood the sheep behaviour pattern in different situations. When they are joyful how they move their bodies and how they express it through their eyes, the same way when they feel fear how they respond. All these reactions show their inner character. Along with external structure knowing their inner character is called … Understanding. "

" I have a question …" She said " as artists we have to show this inner character through their external structures unlike authors who narrate it through words. When we have to express it only through external structure, camera can capture that gesture and expression more easily and accurately than us. If we work our painting from that kind of photograph we will be able to capture their inner character along with external structure. Then why won't our paintings be realistic?

" Yes and No. This is my answer for your question. "

" Please explain sir..."

The same way Giotto understood the sheep behaviour pattern in different situations. When they are joyful how they move their bodies and how they express it through their eyes, the same way when they feel fear how they respond. All these reactions show their inner character.

Your painting won't be realistic. Why?

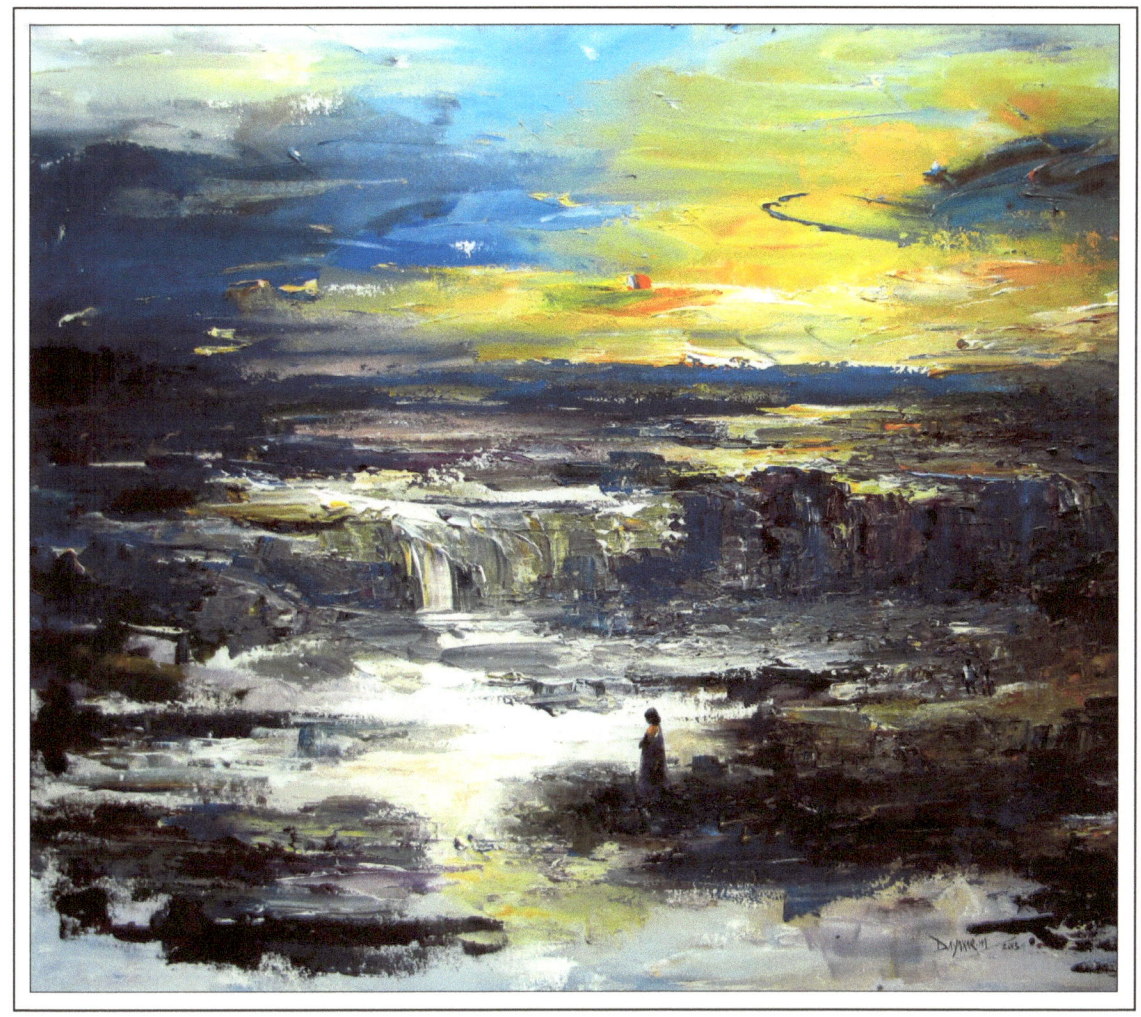

Artist : Magunta Dayakar   Acrylics on Canvas

Why your painting won't be realistic even if you paint it from a photograph which captures inner character of a person or an object?

The reason … the way the eye looks at the things is different from the way camera eye records them. Camera eye records everything whatever it sees without any preferences whereas human eye only sees the things which interests it. It will ignore remaining things.

For example, when a sheep sees the wolf in the distance how it reacts with fear all of a sudden. Does it turn its head up or down or side ways? How the terror reflects in its eyes? How it's body becomes ready to run away from there? How the legs will take the position? And what about the fur on its skin? Is there a movement in the fur due to fear? As an artist you have to find answers for all these questions. Here you have to show the movement just not only in sheep, it should appear in the whole atmosphere. It is a whole.

Your painting is just not capturing the expression of sheep which is in fear. It should be more than that. Your painting is about fear. Life threatening fear in the sheep caused by the presence of the wolf. The whole atmosphere is filled with fear. That is your subject. That is the character of your painting. You have to achieve this character through everything in your painting whether they may be sky, hills, rocks, grass or lambs whatever they may be. You should show the fear of sheep as the dominant theme, other things should be supportive to enhance the expression. Every brush stroke, every value, every color will play a part in this game. A mind game. A game of creativity. This game will make your paintings realistic. This is reality in art. "

I took a pause and asked her … " Now you tell me how is it possible to work realistic paintings from photographs? Yes. You can work from photographs, but you need to add all these efforts to create reality. "

Let's take a look into Giotto's life once again. He was a rural boy and uneducated, living in a village surrounded by hills. His daily routine every morning was to take out the sheep to the hills for them to feed. Once he reached the hills, he did not have anything to do other than watching the sheep, how they look like when they are hungry, How they look at their lambs, how the lambs are hopping, moving around mother sheep, how the mother sheep reacts for its babies sounds, how the male sheep is looking at them, their body fur, the shine of their color in sunlight …. continuing this process day after day, month after month, his senses and mind were wholly absorbed by those sheep attributes, structures, movements ... everything.

Slowly Giotto's mind started to create his own world. In that world he had started to visualise the sheep the way he wanted to see. That's his world. It was created by his vision, his intuition, his insight. You call this as a whole ... A Creative Eye. That eye will penetrate the surfaces, appearances and will go to the soul of the thing or a person.

The people, whoever has achieved great things had this creative eye. To achieve this eye we should learn how to see things as a whole. Key lies there. That is visual imagination. "

Example – Creative Eye

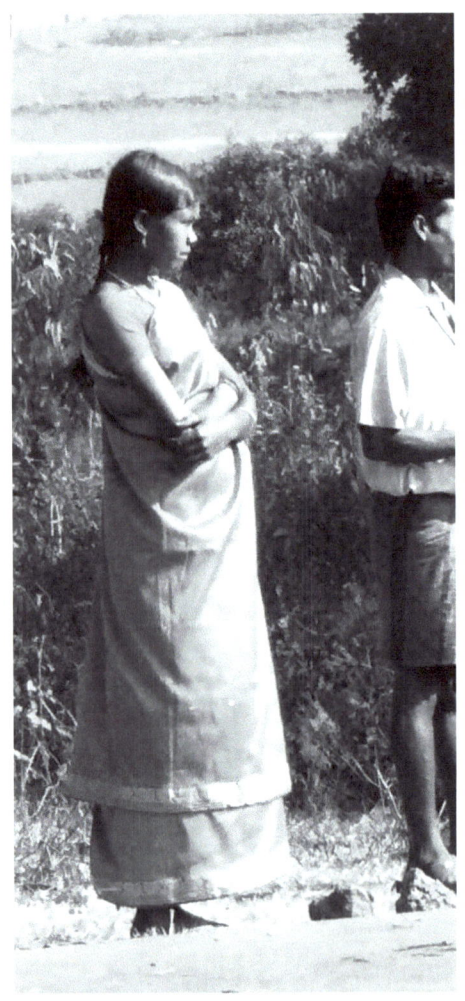

iImage 1

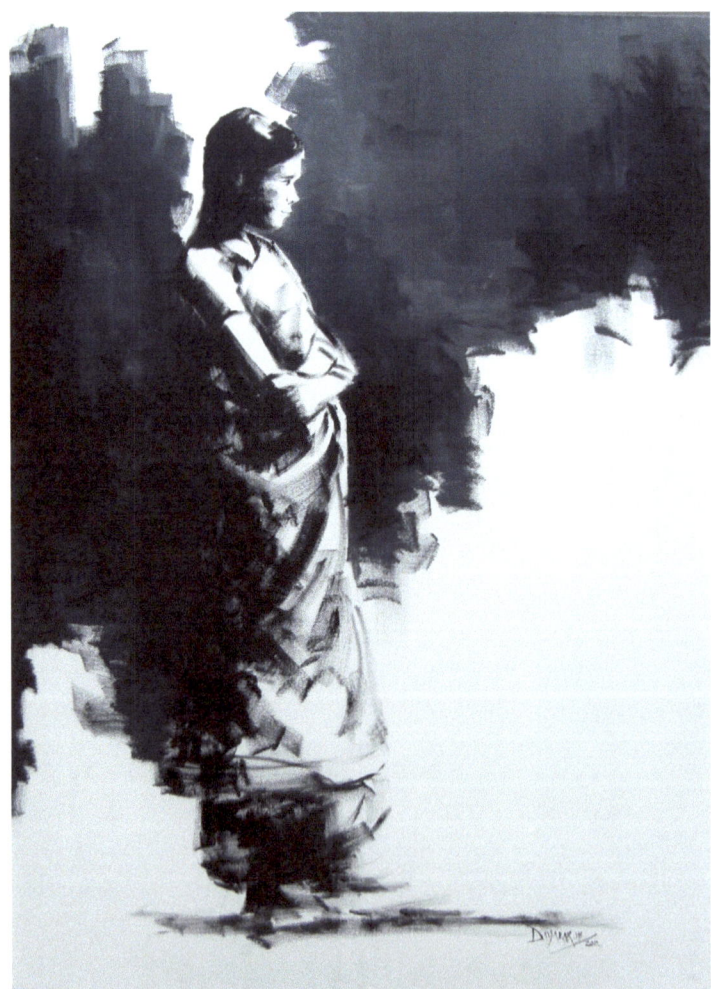

Image 2

Look at image 2. I painted this from the photo which I had taken from a tribal market. I wanted to capture the feeling of movement and serenity. In fact, both movement and serenity are opposites. Where movement takes place, there serenity won't exist. But I would like to achieve it. I tried, and I achieved it by understanding her character.

What is her character? Hers is a small world. Living on the hills, moving with her folks, just struggling for sheer basic necessaries, that's her life. Whenever there's not much struggle to earn basic needs she will be at peace. Other than those moments she would be always in movement like a flowing river.

When I saw her in the market, I understood her joyful state of mind. That is serene. That serenity may end in next few hours. Then movement will happen.

When I feel her serenity and the anticipation of movement in her, I transformed myself into her. It helped me to capture what I want. This is creative eye. This is what Giotto did in his work. Camera will capture the surface structure. Creative eye excludes some of the details in that and will add inner character of the person or subject.

Study the photo and painting, you will understand how I reduced the values in my painting and connected the figure with the background to make it as a whole.

Because of this approach, viewer will feel the serenity and movement in the painting rather than looking at the details of the form.

After finishing the Giotto story, I looked at my student to know her response.

After a few minutes of silence, she asked me, " In class room you used to say that if we love our paintings we will become a failure. From your story what I am feeling is because Giotto loved so much what he is doing, it led to him becoming very successful. Is it not showing that your opinion is not correct? "

" There you are misunderstanding it. He had understood it rather than loving it. That's why he had become successful. "

Chapter Three

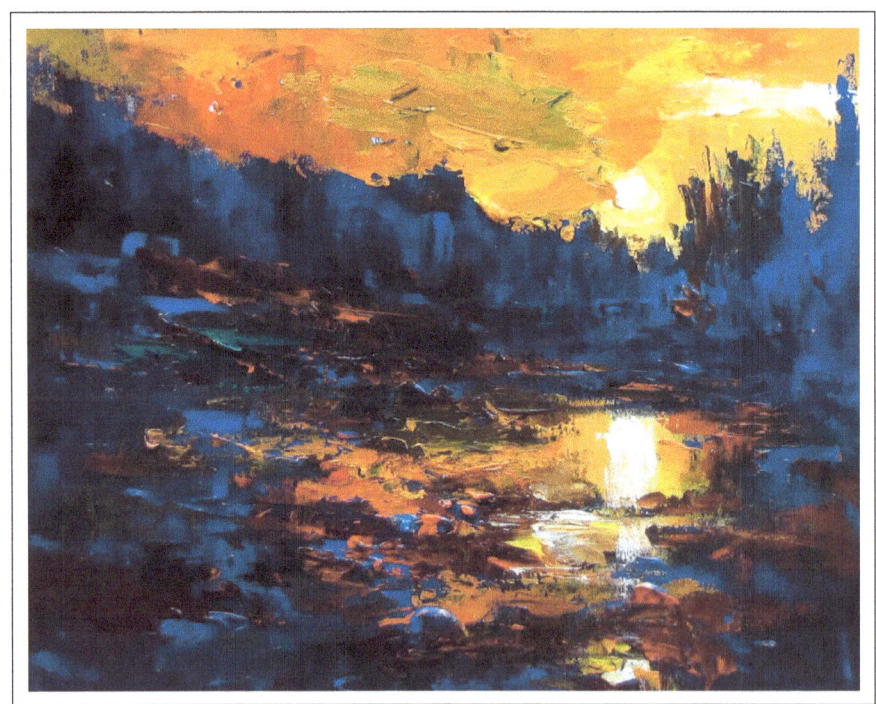

Artist : Magunta Dayakar   Acrylics on Canvas

Love is like a fog. When you are surrounded by it you won't see anything clearly. To see the truth, you have to come out of it.

Rather than loving it

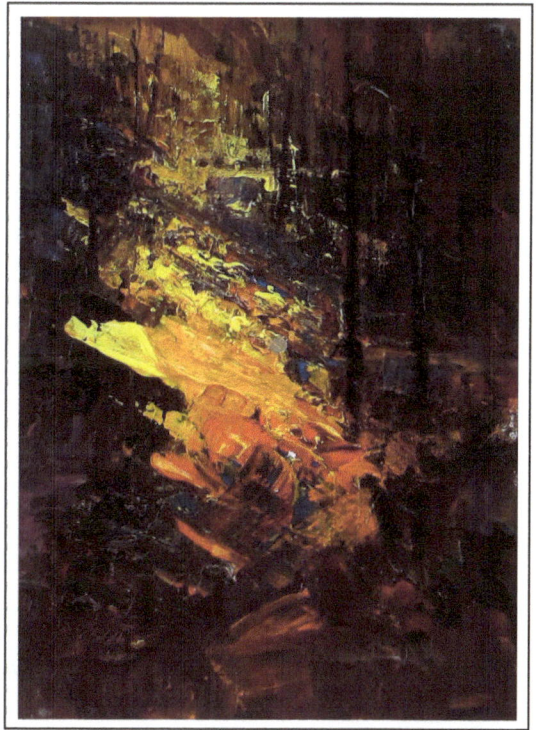

Artist : Magunta Dayakar   Acrylics on Canvas

With surprise in her voice, she asked me. " I don't understand. Is loving different from understanding. When someone loves another one, won't she understand him? "

" Love is different from understanding. Loving something will help you to connect with it with intense passion. Note this word … to connect with it. That is passion or you can call it love. But that's not enough to be successful. You need more than that. Recently one professional artist told me " When someone points out flaws in my paintings, I feel uncertainty. I want to throw

my canvases, brushes and I would like to run away from my studio. "
Actually, he is doing well. Some of his paintings are really good. Even then fear is hunting him. Why?
The reason is LOVE.

When you love something or somebody, what will be the first thing that is going to happen to you?
It is ... Fear!
' You may lose someone you love ' ... that thought itself will create fear in you. You will get shivering. How to overcome that? Only one way is there. To conquer that fear you should not be in love. You should be above it. Then there won't be any fear.
Artists should be like that. They should not love their paintings. Then there won't be any mental agony. No fear. Nothing. This is the right way to become a successful artist.
Confusing! Not loving painting...becoming a successful artist! How can it be? If you don't love your paintings how do you become an artist? ... You may question me.

Not only in art, anyone can become successful in any field, if they don't love their work. Yes. It's true. They will fail, if they love.

You may think ... okay, if you don't love something, you may not feel the fear of losing it. But how do you become successful in a field, for which you don't have any love? It is a puzzle. Is it not?
Yes. It's puzzling. Because, what you have known till this minute is that all successful persons are saying they love their work.
Is it the truth? Really those successful artists or persons are loving their work? Or are they lying? Or maybe they don't know the reasons for their success? To know the truth, these questions have to be answered. That's what I am trying to do. I am searching for the answers.

They say ... Love is Blind. That means the person who is in love won't think about reason. He will be moved by emotions. Sometimes these emotions make him successful, but most of the times they will lead to destruction.

That is love.
Love is illogical. It's not creative also.
A creative mind has to do a lot of search and research. In that search so much analysis is needed. It's logic. All analysis is linked with logic. Logic and love, both are opposite poles. Love never bothers about logic.

I will tell you one incident which happened in a small-time artist's life.

Artists should be like that. They should not love their paintings. Then there won't be any mental agony. No fear. Nothing. This is the right way to become a successful artist.

One incident in a small-time artist's life.

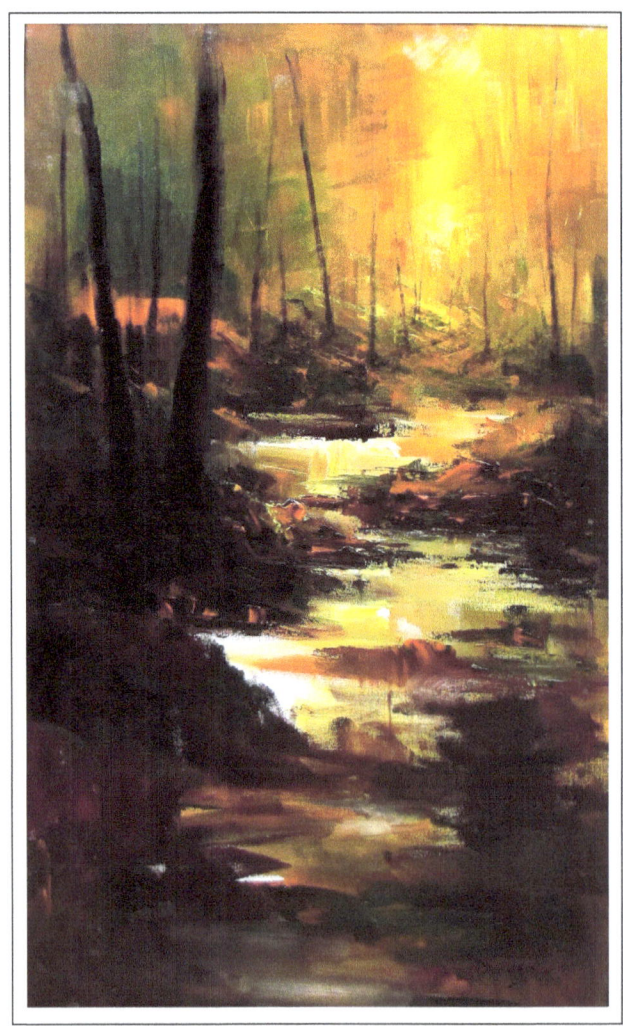

Artist : Magunta Dayakar   Acrylics on Canvas

He is an artist. He does paintings regularly. To him it's a passion. For livelihood, he used to paint sign boards for shops and offices. He is living with some happiness, because he is getting some money for his day to day needs from sign boards and he is doing paintings which he loves very much.

One day someone told him that if he exhibits his paintings in some gallery, he will get some name, then he could sell his paintings to wealthy clients. He would be able earn some good money that way.

He felt it was a good idea.

So he prepared thirty paintings for the exhibition and framed them. It costed him a lot. He didn't have that much money. So he borrowed the money.

After that he approached the galleries which have some name.

Every gallery rejected him. They said they exhibit only paintings of artists' who have fine art degrees and awards.

This artist didn't have any of them. He didn't study in any college. He is self taught. He went to many galleries. His attempts became fruitless.

Finally one gallery accepted his show, with one condition, that he has to pay the rent. He accepted without thinking because he was so excited about exhibiting his works. He thought that he could sell few paintings in his show, with that money he could pay off the rent. He spent some money on invitations and snacks for inaugural day. He borrowed money for that also.

Finally the day arrived.

Invitees came. Some newspapers, one or two TV channel reporters also attended. Everybody praised his talent and the uniqueness of his work. Next day, one or two newspapers and channels published and telecast his work.

He was on cloud nine.

The exhibition was over after five days.

Nobody bought his paintings, not even a single one.

To take the paintings out of the gallery he had to pay the rent but had no money to clear it. Gallery owner told him curtly that he could take out his paintings only after paying the rent. He didn't know what to do. After few hours, he came to the realisation, that he has to borrow some more money to pay the rent to the gallery.

  He borrowed money and took his paintings home.

After few days, he came out of that shock, then slowly started to think …
'He paid money for the invitations.'
'He paid for the snacks. '
'He paid for the canvas boards and colors. '
'He paid for the frames and he paid gallery rent also.'
At the end everybody got their money except him! Is this the actual reality? If it is … why other artists are not speaking about it? Why they didn't warn new entrants like him? Why there's not much talk about artist's struggle for survival? ' So many questions in him. But no answers."

I paused and looked at my student. She is listening very keenly to what I was saying.
I continued again … " Here we need to raise a question, how was this artist influenced by others to put an exhibition to sell his paintings. Why didn't he question, whether people will buy his paintings just because he is putting up a show in a gallery? Why he didn't he ask a few questions to himself?
Question one … Are his paintings good enough for someone to buy?
Question two … Has he established right contacts to sell his work?
Question three … Has he understood the true nature of people's appreciation?
Most people have a tendency, that whenever they see a painting, it does not matter who painted it, they will praise it …" It's good."
It is their good heartedness towards painters. But it is creating a big problem for artist's growth. Most of the artists believe what people are saying is true. What will happen then? They will lose their burning urge to learn. They try to stick to the same work for which people are praising them.

To most of the artists it will happen. Results … Artists are losing their artistic growth. They remain mediocre. What is the solution for this? Be a judge of your own work. This judgement will come with critical analysis. This critical analysis comes with continuous learning.

Here the problem is … If you don't know what you have to learn, your efforts will be wasted in the name of learning. First put an effort to know what you have to learn. Knowing what to learn is the first crucial step for any learner. Here many people go on the wrong path. Remember, your path should be right to reach the destination.

Next ... Don't interact with people for their opinion on your work. They voice their opinions. Most of the times they won't be right. Opinions and facts are usually different. Forget about their existence when it is connected to your work. Try to live, as if though nothing is existing in this world ... except You, Your work and Your learning.

If you don't have money to survive, think of it. No one will survive for long without money. That is the truth, just like how sun rises in the east. Your survival, your art both are different, don't connect them with each other. You are doing painting for your joy. Society does not need to pay for your joy. Don't blame the society because they didn't buy your work. They didn't ask you to learn art. You chose it. But society needs art also like other things. You have to rise to the level where society needs you.

How will it happen? Try to know yourself. Your strengths, your weaknesses ... understand them. Develop your strength continuously, kill your weaknesses mercilessly. This is the way painting has to be structured, this is the way artists have to live, not only artists, every creative person has to live... only this way. I paused for a moment and continued again ....
" Here the problem is ... there is so much talk in the history about artists' struggle for survival. But the problem is, history is talking only about great masters. That means they are successful people to us. Even though they felt pain, starvation, ill health in their life time, in the end they became successful, some maybe after their death. But to an art student who enters into art field, it looks glamorous. Because he is reading about world's greatest artists. To an art student, starvation is not a big deal when he thinks he will achieve great artist status in the end. But after a few years, he would realise that starvation is not a glamorous thing. This world has only a few great masters.
The sad thing is, by the time the artist realises this truth, it would be too late for him ...

The same happened to our small time artist. Influenced by his friends' appreciation for his paintings, he went for an exhibition. Going for an exhibition is not a wrong thing. Before going in to exhibit his paintings to the public he should have known a few things.

One … True strength of his paintings. To know this, he has to study the language of art. But he didn't have that knowledge. So he is not able to judge the strength of his paintings. Without knowing the strength of his work, he believed blindly that his work will sell.

Next thing … who are those wealthy clients buying painting in galleries? What are the factors which will make them buy paintings? This is a very crucial and important point.

Few lines I have heard about Artists

" You are very good at art. " Someone told him in his childhood.
" You are a born artist. " His drawing teacher said.
" What a great artist he is! " His friends praised him.
" God gives that gift only to a few. He is one of those few fortunate people. " The chief guest, one who awarded a memento to him, commented.
" What is the point of this great talent, when it is not useful for survival? " The artist's wife commented.
"… He painted, painted, painted continuously throughout his life even in starvation, ill health and humiliation." Newspapers wrote a few lines on his death.
" What's the point of doing paintings, when you don't know how to sell them? " One artist shouted angrily.
" Even though he was a good artist, his style is not contemporary. ", a critic commented.
" He didn't have the right contacts." One gallery owner stated.

These right contacts are very important to sell your paintings in galleries. These right contacts may be establishing few buyers from your side or having good relations with galleries … In essence, to sell your painting you need good marketing skills along with quality of paintings. Our artist in this story didn't have any of these things. Except love for his paintings. Just love won't work. I am telling you, love only helps to associate with something. From there you have to start your journey with understanding. That will give you success, but our artist stopped his journey just at … Love.

It causes pain to him.

He was shocked with that unexpected pain. It is as painful as when a lover thinks that he is deceived by his love. It's like failure in love. One who fails in love won't think about the causes for it. Simply he blames other one or he blames himself.

Whether it may be true or not, the problem lies with the lover. Why? What's the problem with the lover? The answer is … Before he started to love the other one, he should have understood her nature, her environments, her family and everything about her. But he didn't do any of these. Simply he started to love her overwhelmed by pure attraction. They say it is love at first sight. Where is the understanding here except attraction or desire? When he is not successful at it for some reason, it will cause heart burn. To our artist also same thing happened when he exhibited his paintings, hoping for sales without understanding the realities of that field.

Love is blind. I hope you have understand it from that artist story. It's a proven truth. So just loving your work means you are blind.

Many artists say, " We love our work. We are ready to die for it.''
Maybe! They may die! Anybody moving in darkness without some light, can enter into a dangerous path at any moment. Eventually that will lead to death.

We have seen so many artists who are struggling with their paintings, trying to make them the best. Always they are having doubts about their work. They look nervous. They are seeking opinions from others about how their paintings look. If other person says 'it's good' then they get excited. If they point out some flaws in their work, they will get frustrated. Eventually they will be in depression.

These artists also love their paintings deeply. Otherwise they won't be in depression and frustration. What kind of love is this? Is it helpful to anybody?

Why this is happening?

'It's love'

Loving the work can lead to failures. Depressions. Frustrations.

Again...Why?

Already we discussed this. Love causes fear. Love leads you to reasonless actions. A man without reason, a man full of fear, how can he achieve anything?

A mother loves her child. We love people close to us. Whomever we love, whatever mistakes they do, we will try to ignore their mistakes. If something happens to them because of their misdeeds, we will try to protect them because we love them. In the name of love, we become blind. How can a blind person know the right path?

That's why if somebody says that they love their work, it is idiocy. How can you expect an idiot to become a creator? Idiots can become successful. Success is relative. It's sheerly temporary. Any moment failure can happen.

Vincent Vangogh was not successful in his life time in terms of fame and money. But whatever he created became a great treasure to the world of art. In my view, his life is a great book to the creators. It will tell you how a human being can achieve the greatest things even in misery. That is greatness.

I don't think he loved his work. If he loved his work, today we would not be talking about him. He started to learn painting in his late twenties, he died in his late thirties. During that period also, he did not paint for a few years. Is it not amazing? The man who found a place in the history of art, about whom this world talks after Monalisa, that man, the great Vincent did paintings for a very very short time in his life. But in the end he became great. How did he achieve that? It is by ignoring the society. It is the key. Once he started to ignore the society he became a free man. He didn't need to convince anyone that what he is doing is good. Once he overcame the fear of approval he started to understand the life and what he has to do. By understanding what he has to do he achieved creative eye.

We have been seeing so many artists who are struggling with their paintings to make them the best. Always they are having doubts about their work. They look nervous. They are seeking opinions from others about how their paintings look. If other person says 'it's good' then they get excited. If they point out some flaws in their work, they will get frustrated.

Understanding - Not Love

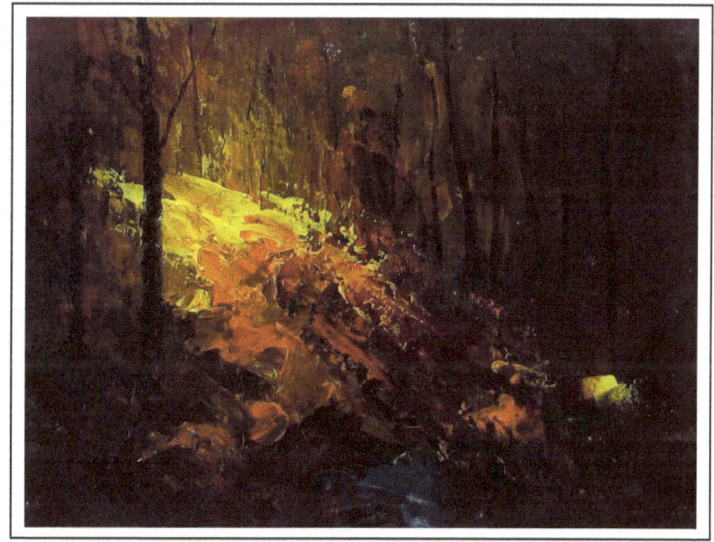

Artist : Magunta dayakar   Acrylics on Canvas

We will struggle to be accepted by society. Why should we bother about society? How do they know what you did is right or wrong? Who are they to judge you? You have to be your own judge. You know your limits. You know your strengths. You know your goals. You should learn what you have to do to reach your goals. Then what is the point, asking somebody to judge your ability. It's meaningless.

They will judge you through their perceptions. Or to their taste. Or through their experiences. When you are depending on somebody to know about you, eventually it leads to frustration. Because they say the things what they feel is right.
Question is, what they are saying, is it right?

I will give you an example to understand this truth. When you are standing on the street in the city you will see only that street. Someone who is looking at the city from fiftieth floor of a tower he will see more of the city than the one on the street. The same way the other one who sees the city from flight window his experience would be different. Ask each of them their experience about the city, each one will give different versions. In fact all are true. From their knowledge they are giving opinions about the city. Judgements of others on your painting are also same. Depending upon their experience they will voice their opinion. They are all partial truths. Those partial truths will push you into confusion. Confusion leads to frustration and depression.

That's why I think all great people never bothered to care others opinion about their work. That's what I understood today, in this moment, when I am typing this, a great truth is revealed to me.
Then what all those great people did for their achievement?
It is ... Understanding. Not love.

When you are doing work without bothering about the end results you don't have any fear because there is nothing you are going to lose. Because you are not expecting anything. Just you are trying to know them both outside and inside. That is understanding. That understanding can make you an adventurous person. A person who is adventurous is above success or failure. Line, texture, shape, size, value, design and composition... learn them but not with love. They can be learnt with Understanding. That understanding will make you a successful painter.

They will judge you through their perceptions. Or to their taste. Or through their experiences. When you are depending on somebody to know about you, eventually it leads to frustration. Because they say the things what they feel is right.
Question is, what they are saying, is it right?

Why artists paint?

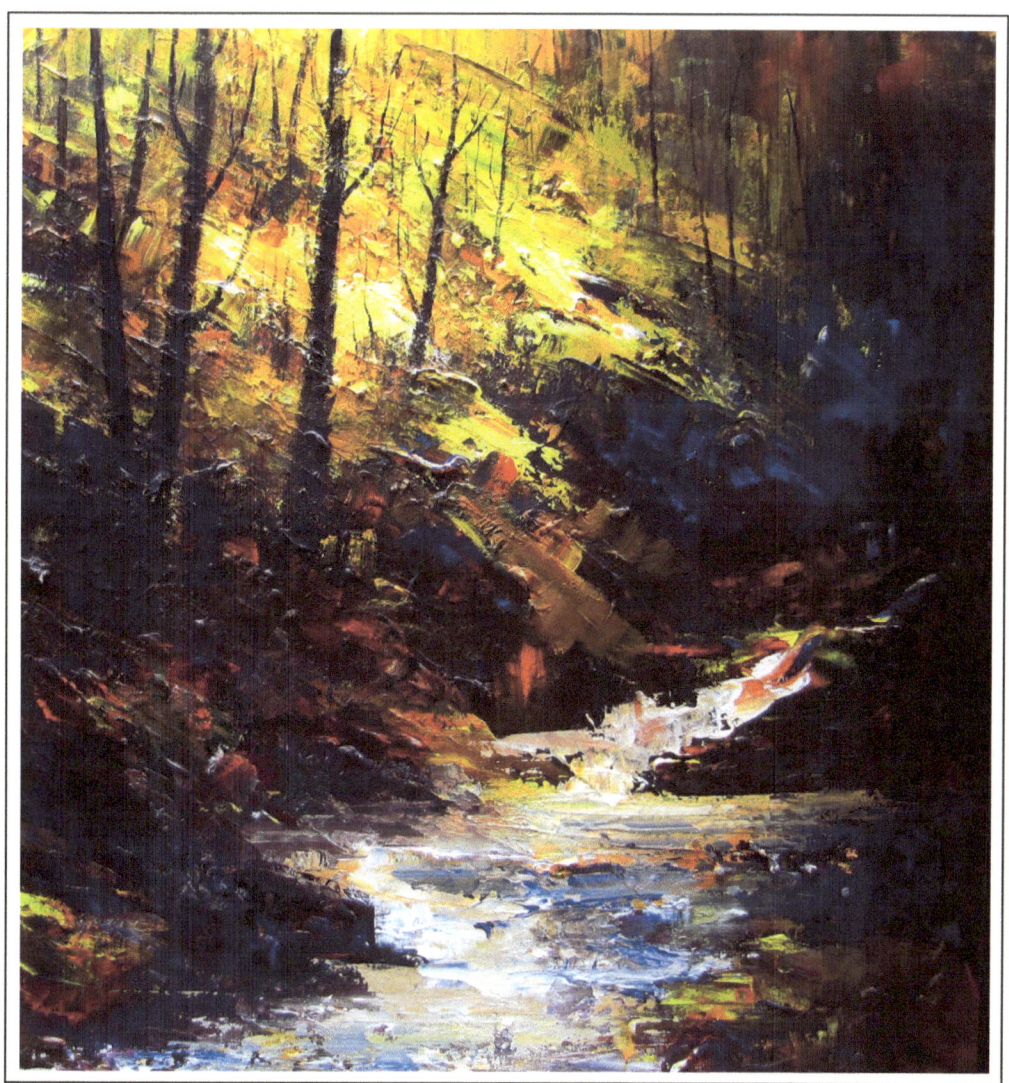

Artist : Magunta Dayakar   Acrylics on Canvas

My student was in silence for some time. Then she asked me. " Sir, one last question … When facing so much uncertainty and insecurity why do artists continue to paint? "

"To live in their soul, they paint. Let me explain. Every human being on this earth will struggle a lot to survive, whether they are poor or rich. If they are poor they will struggle to meet their basic needs, if they are rich they will struggle to grow. Both will struggle for survival, paths may be different. So struggling for survival is a must for any one whoever they maybe, whatever profession they may be in. In that game of survival everyone needs strength to fight.

Same way ... working a painting will test your strength more and more. It is more difficult task than any other. The reason … it's creating life on a two dimensional canvas. If it's not life, it's creating a feeling of an illusion of life on canvas.

Life is precious. Saving life or creating life is priceless. It's invaluable. Even hundreds of millions of dollars cannot save a person from death. Money has no value in terms of life. When an artist has to create life on canvas he should be richer than all the money in the world. Because he is creating life on canvas. But that richness lies in his mind. That richness is … desire to create.

That desire itself is energy. In the universe energy is life. Without that energy there is no life. To create life on canvas, artists will use that energy. In those moments he will explode like a sun. He will feel entire power of the universe in him, at that time.

When that work is over, he will become relaxed but at the same time he starts to feel confidence about his ability to create. To them every painting is a challenge. That challenge tests their strength. If they realize their strength through their work, that will boost their confidence in their ability to survive the obstacles in the journey of life. That is the key ... 'Ability to Survive ...'

From poor to rich, ordinary person to celebrity, everyone needs confidence to survive in life. Most of the people will lose the confidence and strength when problems surround them more and more. Whereas artists will become more hardened day by day with time. Irrespective of miseries they are facing, they will continue their work as if nothing exists in the world except their creative act.

The reason … whenever they are in work, they feel the energy. Energy is life. When a person is getting life from his work, how he could stop it, when life itself is invaluable? That's why … Artists paint not only to create life on canvas but also to feel life, in themselves.

Life is precious. Saving life or creating life is priceless. It's invaluable. Even hundreds of millions of dollars cannot not save a person from death. Money has no value in terms of life. When an artist has to create life on canvas he should be richer than all the money in the world. Because he is creating life on canvas. But that richness lies in his mind. That richness is … desire to create.

My last words

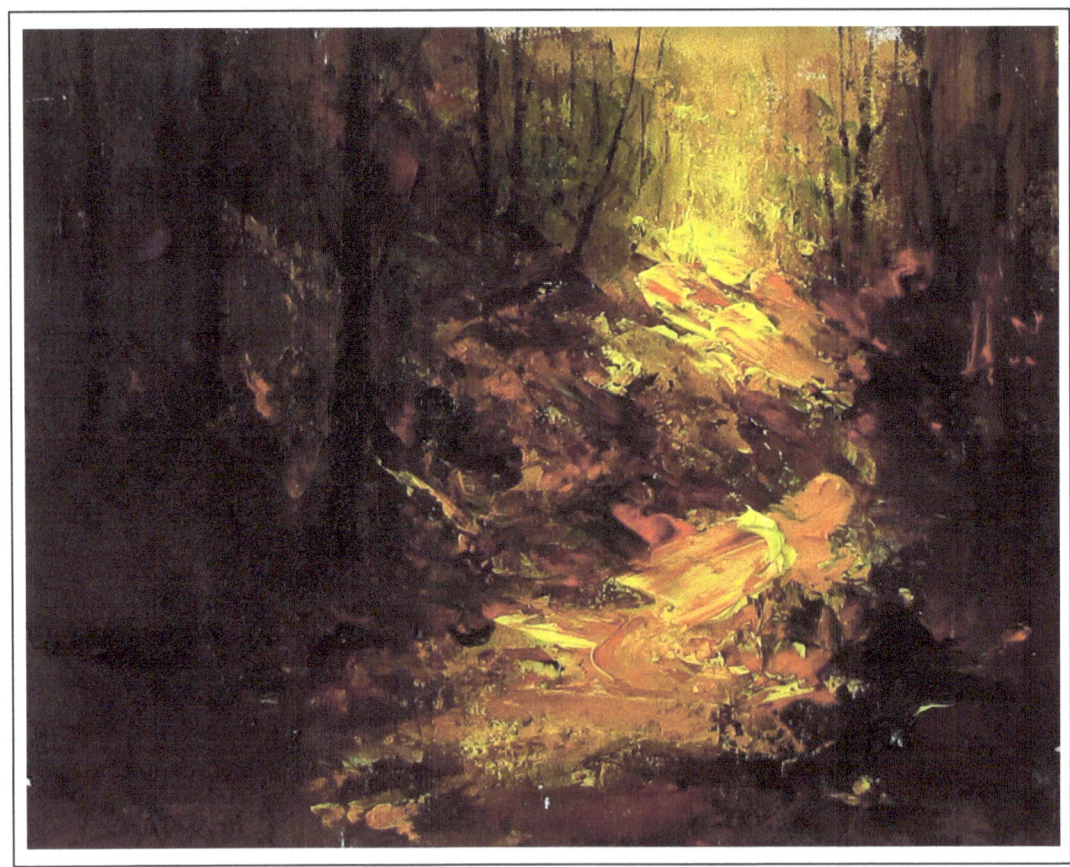

Artist : Magunta Dayakar   Acrylics on Canvas

One day someone asked me..." You are an artist. Do you love nature very much? "
" I don't know "
He paused for one moment, then asked me..." Do you love money? "
" I don't know "
" Do you love beautiful ladies? "
This time I paused for one moment and replied "...I don't know. "
" Do you love your paintings? "
" I don't know. "
He became silent for a moment and then he asked me with a slight irritation in his tone
" Then what do you love? "
" Happiness. " I replied without hesitation.

END

About Magunta Dayakar

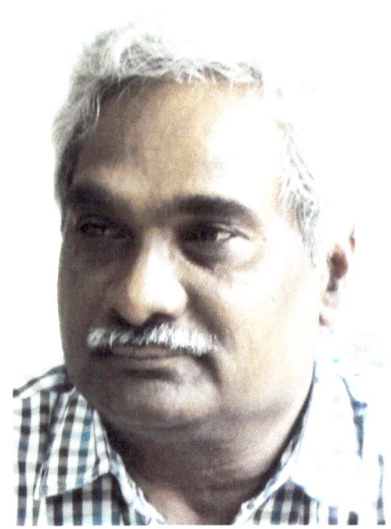

Magunta Dayakar was born in 1951 in Andhra Pradesh, India.
After discontinuing his studies in graduation, he did different things in different periods. He had become a popular fiction writer in his native language Telugu, credited with thirty-five novels. He had worked as an editor and also published a feature magazine for a brief period. He scripted, acted and directed two feature films. He worked for Spectra and Coca Cola India as an artist. He ran Creative Painting School for children in Hyderabad for nearly 15 years.

He believes artist must be able to do all kind of subjects from Still life to Portraits, different styles like Abstract to Realistic Painting rather than limiting himself to one or two subjects and styles, he strongly feels that is the only way any artist will be alive in his journey to understand the Science of Painting.

Now, most of the time he is working on writing books on painting to bring awareness about the Science of Painting. He defines science of painting as …"Just like there are Elements in Nature, there are a few elements in Art also. These elements can be played with using principles (tools) of Composition. Whatever art form you may work with, this knowledge is a must. If not, your work looks like a work of craft rather than a work of art."

Dayakar lives in Hyderabad and is spending all his time with Reading, Writing and doing Paintings. He is not interested in mixing with people, likes only to live with his work other than his family and a few friends.

He says…" Even thousand years is not enough to master the art, so it is meaningless to waste my time with other things. I am not having that luxury. I am destined to understand Art."
He strongly believes what he says and has been living that way.

My website: http://maguntadayakar.com/

My Books on Art
How To Start And How To Plan It ?
How To Finish A Painting ?
Painting Landscapes From Imagination
Learn Composition and Create Beautiful Paintings
Simplified Color Schemes for Art Students
Capturing Movement in Portrait Painting

www.ingramcontent.com/pod-product-compliance
Lightning Source LLC
Chambersburg PA
CBHW051217220526
45473CB00003B/1065